POINTY SIDE OUT:

How to Claw Your Way to the Top (A Feline Self-Help Guidebook)

Dr. Oliver Candelario Carmalita Catman, M.E.C.A.T.

Translated by Kelly Dittmar

PublishAmerica
Baltimore

First printing

ISBN: 1-4137-1572-9
PUBLISHED BY PUBLISHAMERICA, LLLP
www.publishamerica.com
Baltimore

Printed in the United States of America

Dedication

I dedicate this humble tome to the greatest personality I know, me.

—Dr. Catman

The Translator's Acknowledgements

I would like to thank my family and friends for reading the manuscript at various stages, and for offering advice and encouragement. Thanks to George Dittmar and Yoshi Nakayama for photographs.

Special thanks to my husband, Dave, and son, GW, for their love and support. Last, but not least, thanks to Carmalita (a.k.a. Dr. Catman) for his inspiration.

A Cat's Eye View of Life

I know more than most about the trials and tribulations of feline life. I started out humbly enough in a house with three boys. When the family adopted canines, I left on a quest for answers.

I endured stormy winters and hungry nights. I survived cruel humans, fast cars, and fierce wildlife. Fortunately, I was neutered and only responsible for myself.

My journey ultimately took me from the mean streets to easy street. Along the way, I discovered my true calling, which is to help others. I also earned a Doctorate from the local Feline School of Hard Knocks.

This book is the culmination of the life lessons I learned. It is my sincere hope that my humble offering will help other cats achieve their dreams.

Take Action

Your first move is to decide you want to make changes in your life. Once you do that, it takes courage, fortitude, and perseverance to make your dream a reality.

When I started on the path of self-discovery all those years ago, I was scared. I didn't know what would happen. I just knew I couldn't share living space with the flea-bitten dogs my family adopted without my consent.

As I scaled their fence for the last time, I had no idea where my next meal would come from or where I would stay. For me, it was worth the terrible risk.

I lived by my wits, endured driving rain, and ate what I could catch. I was often lonely, hungry, and cold. I lost weight, and my hair became matted and dull.

Then one glorious day I had a vision of what I wanted to do with my life. In my vision, I saw a family in need of fuzzy love. It was a small family with a hamster on its last legs and a boy who needed a cross-species brother. Most importantly, in my view, this family possessed the financial means to lift me from the gutter and give me a new lease on life.

Surprisingly, that family lived on the opposite side of the block from where my quest started. Who would have thought my destiny was so near?

At first, I was simply grateful these people adopted me, fed me, and groomed me. With a full tummy and sporting a newly lush, shiny coat, I saw myself transform.

It was then I knew I could be more than an ordinary cat. I could be a great cat. Purrhaps I could be a leader of cats. During the ensuing five years, I've achieved much and decided to share my good fortune with others.

You, my dear reader, can benefit from my experience and hopefully avoid the pain, suffering, and hunger I endured. Follow my advice, and you too will lead a life of satisfaction, luxury, and fulfillment.

Take control of your destiny and begin your journey of self-discovery. Use this book as your guide, add your own determination, and there is no telling how far you will go.

He who accepts less than the best always gets it.

Me First

Getting what you want out of life takes hard work, dedication, and a keen sense of self-worth. Losers finish last in this world.

Put yourself first. Don't apologize for wanting to better your life.

My approach is simple. It is better to have someone do for you than to do it yourself. Manipulation is an art, not a vice.

Use my proven techniques. Discover why selfishness is a virtue. Learn how to charm your way past mediocrity. And, most importantly, know when to use that quintessential feline asset ~ your rapier-sharp points.

Give someone the chance to make you happy. They probably need the work. I guarantee results.*

---

*Please note: no legal liability intended or implied.

The Purrfect Action Plan

Of course, you must first decide what you want out of life. Only you know what will make you happy.

Begin by setting a goal. It may be lofty or modest. We can't all rule the world, but we can all achieve greatness in our own domain.

Next, make a plan. My worst mistake was rushing forward without first identifying logical steps to take. If I had taken time to plan my move, I might have identified a family to adopt.

After you have some sort of plan in place, take that first step and begin to move forward. Thinking and planning are important, but action is what gets you the prize.

Most importantly, follow through. Good intentions mean nothing if you don't finish what you start.

Finally, reap your rewards. Once you've achieved success enjoy it. It's fine to want more, but don't let that blind you to how far you've come.

Royal Is As Royal Does

Some preach that all beings are created equal. This is just not true. I could cite reams of relevant research, but why waste my time.

We cats are unique in many ways. Did you know that unlike wild feline species, domestic cats' tails remain vertical when we walk? That, despite uncanny peripheral vision, we are unable to see items directly beneath our nose? That from the tip of each ear to the tip of our nose is a purrfect triangle?

If you have doubts we are superior beings, consider this. Why would people cater to our whims, let us out at 3 a.m., feed us expensive tinned fish, and generally let us wreak havoc about the house if we were not gods?

The great Mark Twain recognized the intelligence of our species. He said, "If man could be crossed with the cat, it would improve man, but deteriorate the cat."

It is best to accept that cats are purrfect and to recognize humans need heroes to worship. Be that icon.

If you exude superiority, I dare say, those around you will recognize and reward it.

Exploit your position. Do not apologize for putting others' needs behind your own.

Confidence + Attitude = Power x 2

Like Einstein, I have simplified a complex theoretical paradigm into a simple equation for success. This equation encompasses four universal rules. Follow these, and everything else will fall into place.

1. Never forget you are the best, the tops, *numero uno*, the ruler of your domain.

2. Never allow anyone, especially your human, to forget Rule #1.

3. Be confident. Strut about your territory, point your tail to the sky, and mark all you see.

4. Once you've established complete ownership of your household universe (its contents, occupants, and outlying territories), take a nap. Ruling the universe is exhausting.

One Animal, Two Brains

The complexity of the feline species baffled scientists for years. How, they wondered, did these seemingly innocent, furry creatures become intellectual giants among men?

The inability of humans to comprehend the feline mind is not surprising to the superior being. If they had bothered to ask me, I could have told them. Unlike all other species, we are blessed with more than one brain.

The primary feline brain resides in the cranial cavity. The second resides in our tail.

A cat needs two brains because our body leads a different life from our tail. The head brain orchestrates all intellectual and physiological activity.

The tail brain performs the tasks of a star's personal assistant. It gathers information, it communicates our desires and irritations, and it alerts us to unwanted intrusions.

For example, my head brain calculates the exact length of the rabid neighbor dog's chain during my morning walk. It analyzes which mealtimes and naptimes are optimal. Most importantly, it defines my personality, the traits, quirks, and actions that make me, me.

The tail brain is like a scientific probe or sensor. It collects data and uploads it to the head. There the data is analyzed and actions formulated.

Both brains can operate independently or in tandem. Humans who heed the power of this dual system can generally avoid unnecessary blood loss, pain, and suffering.

Tale of the Tail

One Swish,
Two Swish,
Hello and Goodbye,
Three Swish,
Four Swish,
Run or You May Die.

Nine Lives Is a Cat Food

I hate to inform you that cats have only one life to live. I've traced the origin of the nine lives myth to ancient Egypt.

Ancient Egyptians purportedly revered cats. I dare say, a furry creature living in that desert climate deserved adoration.

Archeological evidence overwhelmingly proves cats were critical to the development of the art of mummification, or "meowmification," as I prefer to call it. The myth of multiple lives evolved over the years.

It is erroneously assumed Egyptians cared deeply for their feline brethren. Little did scholars realize that the size and abundance of our Egyptian ancestors made them the ideal choice for apprentice mummy makers to practice their technique.

The nine lives thing probably resulted from wishful thinking or a simple error translating some ancient stone tablet. The idea just snowballed from there.

My great-great-great-grandcat always said, "I regret I have but one life to give to my species." How true that is.

Remember, it is dangerous, nay, foolish, to believe you have more than one life. Make the most of the time you've got, and by all means avoid busy streets, grumpy dogs, and foul fish.

INDOOR CATS LIVE LONGER

R.I.P.

BUT IN AND OUT THE DOOR CATS HAVE MORE FUN

Ruling Home and Hood

The first task as head of the household is to establish routines for work, meals, and sleep. The length and timing of each of these activities will vary, but remember that humans respond well to strict scheduling and structure.

Today's Schedule

3:30 a.m.	Wake Up
3:35 a.m.	Outside Security
6:00 a.m.	Breakfast
6:30 a.m.	Nap & Plan the Day
10:00 a.m.	Snack & Face Wash
10:10 a.m.	Nap & Monitor House
11:00 a.m.	Visit Personal Office
11:10 a.m.	Bathe & Sleep
12:00 p.m.	Lunch & Window
1:00 p.m.	Nap Master Bedroom
4:00 p.m.	Fish Fry
4:30 p.m.	Visit Personal Office
4:45 p.m.	Bathe & Nap
8:00 p.m.	Snack & Drink
8:10 p.m.	Snooze
9:00 p.m.	Bedtime

Wake Up

I personally like to begin my outdoor work at 3:30 in the morning. My lazy humans are generally lying about in bed at that time, so it takes a bit of effort to get them moving.

My preference is a frantic claw sharpening at bedside. Other times I run back and forth along the vertical blinds. If those attempts don't elicit a quick enough response, I give a couple of warning snorts and pounce on their feet with teeth and claws pummeling.

In extreme emergencies, I lightly swat partially extended points across the nearest nose or gently bite an arm, leaving a bruise but no broken skin.

It has taken some doing, but when that kitchen door opens each morning to the still and dark outdoors, I know deep in my heart I am in charge.

No Snooze Alarm

Huff and Puff,
Huff and Puff,
Cats Who Snort Want Out Now!
Huff and Puff,
Huff and Puff,
Get Up or Claws Go Pow!

Cuisine and Libations

After my brisk morning work, I am mighty hungry. I don't come when called, but the help will.

If my door doesn't swing open promptly at 6:00 a.m., I knock. A good head butt makes a noise that mimics someone pounding urgently at the door.

Inside, I inspect the morning's repast. There is nothing so fine as the aroma of fresh liver paté. I love the velvety smooth texture and complex flavors.

Once sated, I sip from a fresh bowl of cool water. If I am particularly famished, I nibble on some crunchy kibble.

Of course, the beauty of this bucolic scene is much different if the meal is not what was ordered or the water is tepid. If this is the case in your home, do not timidly accept your fate. The most important person in my household, *moi* of course, takes immediate action.

First, I scratch the floor or wall as though burial is what the pathetic offering deserves. I then stare with longing at the great kitchen food box called a refrigerator. Next, I wander aimlessly about the house meowing piteously.

For a dramatic touch, I act weak, thirsty and exhausted. I lick my paws as though they might be my only sustenance.

Don't fret. I won't starve or die of dehydration. Before you can say, "fabulous fastidious furry feline," my human will offer me fresh cold water and a smorgasbord of culinary tidbits.

I never appear too eager or grateful, but I let the help know I am annoyed it took them so long to attend to my needs. I generally emphasize my displeasure with a light swat with points semi-flexed.

These techniques can be utilized for any meal. Remember, if you are offered kibble, demand tuna. If your water is old, refuse to drink it.

This may seem manipulative; it is. Just remember you are a superior being and you deserve superior service.

If you find your humans are not up to the job, you may want to relocate to a more hospitable environment. I tested three households before settling on my latest accommodation.

Cat? Fish Head?

For some reason people call me a "Fish Head." This is a mystery to me. I look nothing like a tin of tuna.

I am a prime specimen of tuxedo clad feline manhood. I'm all dressed up with people to see and places to go.

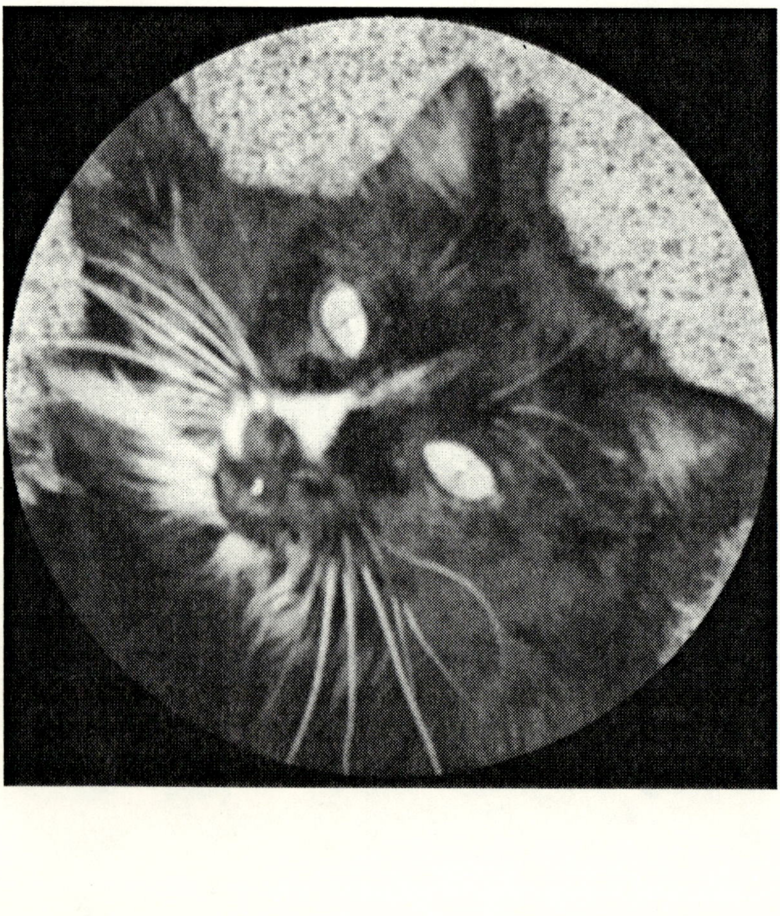

Bedroom Basics

I'm sure you've noticed that sleep is a close second to eating in our daily schedule. The best place to sleep in most households is the master suite.

This is generally the largest bedroom and contains the widest, most luxurious, and most expensive bed. Given my lofty status, this is where I choose to lay my body most days and nights.

Stretching for Space

If you have two head humans in your household, they will likely share this accommodation. Therefore, it is imperative that you stake out a useable space in the middle of the bed. Of course, if you share your home with only one head person, you will split the bed in half.

At bedtime, take a moment or two before your prayers to cuddle with your bedmates. This is the perfect opportunity to position your body horizontally between the two.

I like to think of this as the "H Position." Visualize it. Without your pivotal presence, you would have only a couple of very average parallel lines.

Once the "H" is formed, begin to lengthen your body to fill the entire space. Throughout the night, continue to stretch your body out. Before long, you will have almost the entire mid-section of the bed at your disposal.

I've found that my humans love to sleep on their sides on the very edge of the bed. This leaves a wide comfy space just for me. Of course, once I have the space I need, I generally press my body lengthwise down the nearest back.

Of course if you prefer to sleep at the foot or at the head of the bed, you will choose either the up or down "U Position." If you do prefer the foot of the bed, remember to watch out for the errant kick.

As with the "H Position," the same stretching principles apply. Sweet dreams to you.

Pillow Props

I'm sure you've seen the lush pillows our people use to cradle their heads while they sleep. I've found these are ideal supports for bathing.

I position myself so the center of my back intersects the lower mid-section of the pillow. This allows me to bend and twist without injuring my back while I bathe.

Foam pillows offer the most support. Down pillows tend to squish outward and flatten. Comfort is important when you think about all the grooming we cats do. I personally spend over an hour a day beautifying myself.

The most comfortable spot is always the one occupied by someone else.

Sleeping? Napping? Working?

Few truly understand or appreciate the sleep requirements and habits of the exceptional feline. To the untrained eye we may appear to be lazy lumps of fur, but in reality, we work while we rest.

Most cats need upwards of 18 hours of shut-eye per day. Of this, purrhaps only one-third can be classified as deep REM sleep. The remaining two-thirds I call "closed-eye wakefulness."

I'm not sleeping, I'm planning the day's agenda. It is during this important time I combine rest, planning, and security activities. Even with eyes closed, I write schedules, monitor the help, and track canine marauders.

I like to think of myself as a fur-clad computer, or a fuzzy byte o' mainframe. Either way, I am rarely off the job.

Cuddling for Profit

Cats come with two sides: the cuddly, furry side and the business side, otherwise known as the pointy side. The cuddly, furry side uses purrs, nudges, and soft whisker kisses to induce humans to do our bidding. Once mesmerized by fuzzy love, it is easy to impose your will on the unwary.

I personally use this technique to get special treats, get my itches scratched, and persuade my people to buy me catnip and tinned fish. I find it is especially effective on cold, wet mornings when I just want my feet and buttocks warmed.

I also use this cuddle technique to jockey for position in the big bed at night. People will generally make room for a purring kitty when they expect a little loving.

At this point, I position my furry self in the middle of the bed near the pillows. For some reason, people find it is against their nature to dislodge a cuddling cat. On cold nights, I slip my body under the covers as we snuggle, and then I snooze away as warm as toast.

You will find that cuddling helps your human as well. It makes them feel nurtured, loved, and needed.

I think of it as feline charity work. Cuddling may be a calculated act, but the time involved is a small price to pay for the rewards we gain in the end.

If I want company, I will look you up.

Cuddly Credit Plan

At times, every feline needs expensive food, playthings, or medical care. Of course, one can't always predict what or when, so I plan ahead.

I cozy up to the person in my household with a fistful of plastic and the highest credit line. When a crisis or personal need occurs and my special credit-worthy buddy whips out that beautiful, little, rectangular consumer fulfillment aid to pay without hesitation, I know I have done my work well.

Do not view this as a mercenary act. Give your human the opportunity to make you happy and keep you healthy. It gives them a warm and fuzzy feeling inside and makes them smile.

Getting what you need or want is what's important here. Needless to say, I sleep well all day, and all night too, for that matter, especially when I'm on my expensive, ergonomic, faux-leopard sleeper.

Points to Ponder

Sometimes, however, the cute, sweet act fails to achieve the desired result. Then it's time to flex the points. The use of our razor-sharp claws is a matter of personal preference, experience, and, ultimately, the urgency of our need.

Some felines consider the use of points a last resort. Needless to say, I do not subscribe to this pacifistic approach. I am a humanist. I love to scratch humans.

I strongly believe that if you spare the point, you spoil an opportunity to get your way. Remember, our claws are one of the greatest God-given tools on the planet. Use them.

There are several strategies I employ. Only one involves bloodletting. Once I've got my person's attention, I show them what I need (cold water, a fluffy pillow, a treat, etc).

Stretch Pause Claw (SPC)

The SPC method is especially effective if you have an audience. Do remember that noise is your best friend. When humans hear scratching, they naturally fear the worst.

First, find the most expensive piece of furniture in your home. Casually walk to it. Locate the most visible portion, and slowly stretch your lithe body out.

Reach upward, pause for a count of five and deploy frontal points. Scratch at will. I dare say people can fly, given the right circumstances.

Bare Flesh Caress (BFC)

This is another excellent tactic. Locate the most sensitive person in your household. I prefer to approach the head female and act as though I am in need of a good cuddle.

After a brief sweet interlude, I locate a bare patch of skin (preferably on the arms or face) and gently place the soft pads of my paw and partially deployed claws on the tender epidermis. Hence the BFC moniker.

I purr softly while I am making this move. It lets my human know I just want immediate attention and that I prefer not to cause permanent damage. Of course you can't be afraid to up the ante if needed.

Stealth Jump (SJ)

This approach gets the best response at night. Slip into the master bedroom, slither across the floor silently, and pounce.

I prefer a stomach landing, points down. The additional fatty tissue on the average person's mid-section cushions the landing, I've found. Since the SJ is the equivalent to launching a sack of potatoes into someone's gut, I reserve this method for dire circumstances only.

Old Fashioned Bloodletting (OFB)

In any case your last resort is to draw blood. No instructions needed here. An OFB comes naturally to us felines and requires no preparation or restraint.

No need for guilt here. To my knowledge, no one ever bled to death from a cat scratch. Just in case, apply firm pressure to the wound.

Word of the Day:

Ailurophobia: the abnormal fear of cats

(Purrhaps it is just the fear of our points?)

Life's Trials

Let's face it. There are many nasty trials we felines face daily. Some inconveniences like closed doors, hairballs, or a dirty litter box can be expected on a regular basis.

Others crises, such as nationwide kibble rationing or roving raging dogs may be rare. Emergency plans need to be in place to minimize the impact, should an unexpected crisis occur.

Closed Doors

Curiously, I've discovered that closed doors attract cats like magnets. In the still of the night, doors can block access to the choicest sleeping locale, the master bedroom. Never fear, the soft squishy bed need not be out of reach for long.

First, I meow sweetly as a gentle reminder that the master of the domain is locked out. If the "open sesame" approach doesn't work, I jiggle the base of the door with my paw while meowing in increasing volume.

On those nights when no amount of coaxing works, I alternate loud cries, head butts, scratching and jiggling. Few can ignore this for longer than a few minutes.

Once the door cracks open, I shoot through and settle in the middle of the bed. With my motor setting on high, I rely on cute fuzzy love to defuse any lingering anger. As we drift off to sleep, I rest assured I am the center of my universe, if not at the center of my king size bed.

The savvy cat will use these methods anytime of the day or night. You don't even have to be taking a nap or going to bed. You may just be curious about what lies on the other side. The pillows always are softer behind a closed door.

Hair Today, Hairball Tomorrow

Hairballs, those cylindrical wads of regurgitated feline body hair, which pop out of our mouths regularly, are distasteful to say the least. When you feel the need to expel coming on, let the whole world know.

Our families must experience the inconvenience of hairballs right along with us. I call this "equal suffering"; if I must suffer, so shall you.

Make it a point to make as much noise as possible while you are working the hairy clump to a quick exit. For maximum impact, do this in the wee hours of the morning while all is quiet, except for you, of course.

When the inevitable occurs, find a special place for your deposit. Hide and Seek is not just a children's game. It is a game of strategy and cunning when hairballs are the subject.

Your secret place can be planned in advance. Purrhaps in an expensive shoe deep in the darkest reaches of the closet, or on the Persian rug in the formal living room.

Once the furry link is out, walk nonchalantly away and wait for the show to begin. Your human will stumble forth from the warmth of their bed and search high and low for the mess. If you've done your job well, they will conclude it was a false alarm and crawl back to bed.

Hours, days, or even weeks later, someone will detect that something is not quite right. Once reality sinks in, there will be an outburst, so be prepared.

To soften the blow, curl up in the warm sunshine and let the golden glow do its work. Your angelic aura will probably distract your human long enough to defuse their loud promise of violence, and you will likely be in for a sweet cuddle. If it's cloudy or dark, however, forget angelic and hide.

Household Cleaning Tip:

Use special pet paper towels with plastic coating on one side to pick up hairballs and other nasty spits.

Hairballs: Part II

As you know, hairballs have a mind of their own, and there are times you will not be able to implement your planned depository agenda. If you find yourself in this situation, your best alternative is volume. This refers to both noise and quantity.

I try to position myself in the middle of the most trodden pathway in my home. I prefer an area that is carpeted and difficult to clean.

Next, I expel as many hairballs as possible in a neat row. My personal best is four links. This tactic generally arouses great interest. It insures the mess will be discovered promptly and disposed of quickly.

In any case, it is imperative to make yourself scarce. Find a warm place to nap for a few hours, especially if someone steps barefooted into the still warm mess.

RECYCLING TIP

CRAFTY FOLK WEAVE MITTENS FROM FURRY KITTY SPITTIN'S

Litter Box Follies

We cats are fastidious creatures. We hate to smell, we hate to be dirty, and we especially hate an overloaded litter box.

I dare say, our offices should be emptied after each use, but most of us don't live in a luxury penthouse with staff. Most litter boxes are cleaned every other day at best.

I must admit that those fabulous new litters and crystals have their olfactory benefits, but wading through a swamp of yesterday's waste is unsanitary, not to mention, demeaning. Our humans forget the paws fouled by the unmentionable will touch furniture, counters, and most importantly, our sweet lips.

If the maid or butler in your suite is not paying proper attention to your bathroom, you may have to resort to certain measures to get it cleaned.

The least offensive method I use to alert my caretaker is to meow piteously while I sit upwind of my office. Of course, if the desired cleaning takes place, I reinforce good behavior and step into my box immediately.

If this doesn't work, try artistic means. I try to find an expensive rug, bedspread or article of clothing with a suitable brown background. I like to use Daddy's side of the bed. It lets him know I am thinking about him while he's at work.

For maximum effect, I do my temporary artistic installation when no one is home. I form what I call "pooart." I choose a recognizable object. I use the pyramid: it symbolizes energy and power, and it is especially easy to shape.

Once the deed is done, walk away. If you've made the right background color selection, your work will have its greatest impact.

In any event, your litter box will be sparkling clean before you know it. Again, a quite nap in an out of the way locale is the purrfect finale.

Caution:

Beware of motorized litter box contraptions. The tail you save might be your own.

Survival Skills

Keep your hunting skills and claws sharp. You never know if you might run out of kibble, or be tossed to the elements. The work you do today could save your furry behind from untimely extinction.

Razor Sharp Claws

Claw sharpening comes naturally, so just go at it. Remember the wooden legs of a table are just like the trunk of a tree.

The older the tree, the more seasoned the wood. The better the wood, the sharper the claw.

Antique is just another word for old wood. Most homes have an abundant supply.

Newspapers are purrfect for testing if claws are razor sharp, but only if the paper hasn't been read yet. Go forth and sharpen.

Indoor Safari

Hunting opportunities abound inside every home. I find the early morning hours ideal for this type of work. First, cats are generally awake, and second, you have a captive audience to witness your prowess.

By dawn's early light, patrol hallways, under beds, and in the deepest, darkest closet corners. This is the natural habitat of the eight-legged species, *Arachnidas Hujicus*.

Hujicus is oblivious to noise, so there is no need to stifle your approach. In fact, noise will alert your family to the vital security work you are doing.

Once you have located prey, study its movements and plan your attack. This interlude will generally give your humans time to gather as well.

When the audience arrives, pounce and devour the large, dangerous creature with a resounding crunch. I dare say, "hero" is a word one can't hear enough.

If the local exterminator has eliminated this prey from your habitat, your next option is to hunt the wily *Dusticus Bunnicus*.

This wispy looking creature lurks under beds and other large pieces of furniture. Approach with caution.

Outdoors

If you are outdoors, avoid hunting birds and other pretty prey. Bird catchers are labeled kitty killers and punished accordingly. Rodents, bugs, and other unwanted pests are fair game.

These practice sessions will keep your skills sharp. In the event you get locked out or tossed out, however, my best advice is to find an open window at the house next door. My neighbor's garlic chicken beats cold mouse any day of the week.

A Word of Advice:

With all this nocturnal hunting, shredding, and claw sharpening, there is the potential kitty will be punished on some trumped-up charge.

If your family is not appreciative of your work, you can avoid serious consequences by following this advice. Punish yourself first.

I know it sounds harsh, but if your family is already mad, isn't it better you voluntarily go to kitty time out? I like to think of this as a strategic preemptive strike.

I personally sit under a table, chair or other large object and look appropriately contrite. This move generally startles your people. They are not used to seeing kitty admit to anything, but being superior.

Often they assume you've already learned your lesson, and that is that. If, however, someone is armed with a broom, run!

Inclement Weather

Wind, rain, snow, and heat may not stop our faithful public servants from delivering the mail, but they wreck havoc with us felines. If you are an "in-and-out-the-door" cat, you will need to establish bad weather rules. If you are a full-time *al fresco* cat, I pity you.

Mother Nature equips cats with special weather sensing tools. Feline brains, ears, and eyes provide the first line of defense.

If you hear trees creaking and bangs against the house, or if you see the dog fly by, it's a windstorm. If all you see is water pouring down, it's rain. If there is ice, snow, or hail, it's cold. If your kibble melts, it's hot.

Cold Weather Cautions

Each fall, I monitor the growth of my purrfect mane and the length of the hair between my soft and supple paw pads. Copious amounts of hair indicate a bad winter season ahead.

The greatest danger in cold weather is hypothermia and frostbite. The most vulnerable body parts are our ears, noses, bottoms, and paws.

If you must spend time outdoors or you are tossed to the elements, have a survival plan. My first choice is to bunk with the neighbors. They are always thrilled I want to visit, so I take advantage of their hospitality on cold days. Otherwise, seek out dry spots under bushes, dryer vents, or warm car hoods.

When it's icy, remember that firmly flexed points serve as traction devices on walkways and windowsills. One winter, I fell headfirst into a snowdrift after sliding off my ice-glazed sill. Now I'm prepared.

While you are outside, keep your eyes and ears open at all times. As soon as you hear someone touch the doorknob, position yourself to shoot through to the warm indoors.

Once inside, find the closest lap and warm your toes and bottom, or park yourself in front of a furnace vent and let the warm air work its magic.

Keep Your Cool

Hot summer days need not threaten life and limb. Modern environmental control tools include frozen gel packs, electric fans, and air conditioning. Use all the tools available to you, and you will be cooler than a cucumber in an icehouse.

On hot days, plan to stay indoors and move as little as possible. This is not too difficult, since we cats are second only to the sloth in our need for sleep.

If your home has central air, lie back and enjoy the vibe. If it does not, a cool gel pack tucked under the buttocks works wonders.

I personally prefer to combine a ceiling fan, a dark room, and a cold gel pack for a relaxing, spa-like rest. I hate to admit it, but if all else fails, a good dunking is your only alternative.

Of course, never let the help see you looking cool and rested. It demoralizes them to see you suffering from heat.

As a result, they will redouble their efforts to make you extra comfortable and will likely bring a bowl of iced water and a tray of cold fish to your bedside. Enjoy.

Overheated

I'm Hot, I'm Parched,
Don't Want to Move,
Bring Cold Drinks
and Fishy Food.

Emergencies

In the event of extreme situations, run and hide. Survival equals eight-tenths paranoia and two-tenths preparation.

I have a personal bunker in my basement that I use when faced with booming fireworks, loud sirens, and wild animal packs. Outdoors, I favor a window well, tall tree or dense bush.

The best shelters have easy access to food, water, and bathroom facilities. I also store at least three weeks worth of tuna and kibble rations, 50 pounds of litter, and a case of bottled pure spring water. I suggest you do the same.

As far as other emergencies, all I can recommend is that you expect the unexpected and plan for the unthinkable. If you are lucky, you will survive. If not, it was nice knowing you, and I thank you for buying my book.

Time Off for the Help

Every so often, your humans will beg for a vacation from domesticity. People really love to lounge about, so sometimes they need time to themselves without having to respond to feline demands.

The length of these vacations could be anywhere from a few hours to a few weeks. Trips longer than 48 hours generally require some type of in- or out-of-home care.

I prefer to be home myself. I am a people person. I need people to pamper me.

I've discovered that if you have the right reputation in the hood, the local vets will not welcome you to bunk in their kennel facility. This is just as well. Who wants to spend copious amounts of time in the same space as dogs, rats, or other sad sack creatures?

When I was younger, I stayed with the neighbors. On the days I needed a room for the night, I met them on their front stoop as they came home from work.

I'd remain in their home as an honored guest for as long as needed. When my family got home, I packed up and left.

Now that I am an elder statesman, I prefer to remain in my own luxury suite rather than schlep to the neighbors. So I use a live-in nanny for vacations.

In any case, make friends with your caretaker, even if it is the local vet. This is the one time I advise you to spare the point and stem the tide of blood.

Snuggle frequently with your human helper and purr non-stop, except when you are alone. Your caregiver will think you are adorable and offer you the freshest food, the choicest treats, and keep your office sparkling clean.

After my last vacation, Nanny Jila told my family, "Kitty has been a joy. He liked to watch TV with me and just wanted to be loved." How true it was.

Revel in the attention; it won't last forever. Enjoy your vacation as much as your humans will theirs.

When your family returns, do not jump eagerly into their arms. Of course they will have worried that you suffered in their absence. Do not let them know that you did not suffer for one minute.

Use their guilt to your advantage. Plan to ignore them for the first few hours (take a nap or just go outside and sit), and when they try to snatch some fuzzy love, swipe at them with a partially flexed paw.

Act nonchalant about any gifts they give you. In the mean time, decide what you want in exchange for the suffering you supposedly endured.

If their vacation was longer than four days, the sky is just about the limit. I ordered a new faux-leopard pillow after one two-week vacation ordeal.

Hours later, you can enjoy a good cuddle and let them know all is forgiven. Just do not act like you missed them too.

I know waiting is hard, but you have to consider your social position and your reputation in these situations. After all, the whole point is that superior beings do not grovel for attention from lesser beings.

The Vet

Good veterinary care may be key to longevity, but it doesn't mean anyone has to enjoy it. Syringes, thermometers, and scalpels represent the medical torture arsenal. Sharing space with canines adds to the horror.

When you see your personal transportation carrier retrieved out of the dark reaches of the basement, run and hide. The height of the space underneath the largest bed bars the smallest human, so lodge your body beyond arm's reach. Bared teeth, flexed claws and hissing let your intentions be know.

If your human reaches you with a grabbing device or blocks your planned escape route, your only alternative is a bloodletting. They may succeed in locking you in your cage, but they will wish they had taken out stock in first aid supplies beforehand. Don't worry. Scars fade, and wounds heal.

On your way to the vet, meow as though doomed, and alternately pant, hiss, and howl. Pet carriers are especially hard to carry when the load keeps moving. Shift positions frequently and swat at any flesh near the bars.

In the doctor's reception area, maintain a low profile. No need to alert the dogs or other animals of your presence.

Once in the exam room, your helper will try to comfort you and probably set you free. Use this opportunity to slither under a chair or behind a cabinet and plant your hindquarters against the wall.

When the vet arrives, refuse to move and threaten anyone who attempts to dislodge you. If you are overpowered, bite and scratch at will. If you are lucky, you will be labeled a vicious cat, and the vet will ban you.

If this does not work, submit only to a cursory once over. Do not turn your back on anyone, or you may have a thermometer rammed up your buttocks to check your temperature.

The last humiliating step will likely be shots of some sort. Fortunately, shots are generally quick and painless. When it's time to go, give the vet a goodbye swat and hop into your carrier.

From the Desk of Dr. Catman

Dear Dr. Vet,
Please read and sign the attached liability waiver. It absolves me of responsibility for pain, blood loss, or scars, should you poke or probe within six feet of my furry body.

Dr. Catman, M.E.C.A.T.

Overnights

Most veterinary visits last less than 20 minutes. If, however, you are injured or purrhaps getting permanent birth control, your stay will be longer and may involve surgical procedures.

My only advice here is to scratch, howl and claw your way to a private room. There is nothing worse than feeling crummy and being stuck in a cage next to a mangy dog in for a triple flea dip.

Medicine

Sometimes your doctor will give you a prescription. In my case, I refuse to swallow a pill. Hence, I get liquid in a dropper.

Unfortunately, it is never fish flavored. Once I got pink bubblegum. With more than half a billion cats in this world, you would think that they would cater to our tastes once in a while.

Anyway, when it's time for my medicine, I am nowhere to be found. I am in a hard to reach spot watching two grown adults crawl around looking under furniture.

One carries the medicine dropper carefully so as not to spill any of the precious liquid. The other is wearing gloves, armor, kneepads, and is carrying a towel and muttering bad words under his breath.

Once the screaming, bleeding, and fur stops flying, I find myself wrapped in a towel, like a burrito, with fingers prying my lips apart. At this point, it's easier to let them squirt the medicine in my mouth.

I quickly spit it out while shaking my head vigorously. Generally, they give up exhausted and just unroll me and clean up. After rinsing my mouth, I take a long nap.

Aging Gracefully

We cats go through many physical changes as we age. Sometimes I hear unfounded comments regarding the graying of my luscious coat and the whiskers on my chiseled chin.

To those, I say these are not gray hairs, but wise hairs. I am not old and gray, I've ripened.

I do notice, however, napping is becoming an increasingly important pursuit. I find I especially enjoy a cushy electric blanket on cold nights. I also prefer warm milk to sour milk on Saturday night.

I do, however, deny allegations that I've slowed down. I've observed that the rodents, birds, and butterflies run and fly faster day by day.

I am certain the thinning of the ozone layer is to blame here, however. I've secured a multi-million dollar government grant to study the issue. I hope to have answers before the next millennium.

Of course, although I am confident my untimely demise is many years and purrhaps decades away, I have completed plans for my own funeral services and granite memorial statue. It is fair to say my presence won't be forgotten for many generations to come.

My best advice to you is to avoid discussions about age. I've been lucky that since I've switched families several times, no one is certain of my age. I'm not telling. Also, remember to cavort like a kitten, live for the moment, and don't forget that nine lives is a myth.

123456789LIVES

IS A MYTH

Neighborly Relations

Unfortunately, we do not live in isolated environs and must share space with others. In case you hadn't noticed, there are people, animals, and insect creatures living all around us. Those who are not in your immediate family are called "neighbors."

Marking your territory helps others identify your domain. Unfortunately, some neighbors, in particular other felines and canines, will dispute boundaries and try to claim your land as their own.

Dealing with these intrusions requires daily security work. Neighbors who just want to share a sunny step or sit under a smelly flower bush are easily tolerated. I say live and let live. I am a generous cat and willing to share space, but do not presume to claim my territory as your own.

In those situations, confrontation may be your only defense. Of course, I try to learn as much as I can about my rival before taking such action.

As you know, some fierce kitties are small and wiry, and some gentle dogs are big and slobbery. Never assume your neighbors pose no threat. "Caution first" is my motto.

In the past, I paid dearly for ignoring that simple credo. A local she-devil moved into my hood and quickly staked out my territory.

In haste, figuring a girl was no match for my testosterone, I launched into a fight. Before I knew what hit me, I was splayed out with a nasty gash on my forehead, a newly pierced toe, and a battered bladder.

Days later, after rest and an expensive hospital stay, I decided to share space with this behemoth. I arranged opposite working hours to avoid unnecessary contact. Needless to say, she was less than the ideal neighbor, but we learned to co-exist by alternating indoor and outdoor activities.

I dare say, she would have loved to evict me, but that was not going to happen to the king of Proctor Street. I simply chose to go to work from 3:00 a.m. to 6:00 a.m. and avoided all times she was outside.

This same tactic works for other pesky beasts. The important thing is to hold your tail high and diligently scent your way through the hood. I like to tank up on liquids in the evening so I am fully loaded and ready to go when out on patrol.

Anyway, be good to your neighbors, and they may be good to you. At least they will tolerate your using their garden as a potty, if they think you are a decent sort.

If you have a bad attitude, however, do not expect any latitude when it comes to the neighbors tolerating your visits. When in other yards watch out for booby-trapped gardens, unleashed dogs, and little sticky people, otherwise known as children.

If I live next to you, I am a neighbor.
If I live with you, I am family.

Pesky Pests

Billions of pests inhabit this world. Some are deadly. Some are unsightly. Some come in swarms. And, some are just plain nasty.

I selected four I find particularly annoying. Depending on the region in which you live, you may have other pests that pester you more.

The noisy din of bugs, dogs, birds and kids
makes me want to stay in bed.

Fleas

There are millions of fleas in the world. I have it on good authority that over 75% prefer delicate feline blood to sour canine blood. I certainly would if I were a flea.

If you enjoy outdoor strolls, I suggest you speak to your vet about monthly treatment options. The temporary effects of topical pesticide outweigh the humiliation of being a flea ferry port to port.

Yappy Dogs

Have you ever noticed that the smaller the size of the dog, the louder and shriller its bark? If they were not so noisy, I would enslave one to do my bidding.

Picture me on a chaise lounge being fanned by the beast and sipping iced tuna water while listening to the Stray Cats. I would be a happy man.

Unfortunately, that is not acceptable in our current social climate. So, I'm developing a treatment to mute these noisy beasts.

So far, a noose system seems most effective, but there are some unpleasant side effects. I'm back to the drawing board.

I plan to test a new design soon. My Stifle Muzzle prototype looks promising, but let's just keep this our little secret for now.

Avian Dive Bombers

Every spring, a husband and wife team of jays invades the air space in my territory. This prolific pair breeds little jay pests by the bucket.

The incessant chirping of these baby jay rats is not the source of my ire. It's the psycho parents who bedevil my day.

Picture me walking next to my fence in dawn's early light. Before you can say "Alfred Hitchcock" those two are hopping along the top of the fence screaming to wake the dead. Without further warning, the dynamic duo make alternating bomb runs at my furry head.

If not for quick thinking on my part, I dare say, they would peck my eyes out. I evade their attack under the closest lawn furniture. A lounger works best, but in a pinch, a side table will do.

I suggest you glance skyward frequently when outside. Birds are masters of the stealth approach. I just hope my tormenters move to Bermuda next year.

Inquisitive Children

There is nothing so tempting to unruly rug rats than a kitty napping in the sun. Before you can flex a claw or bare a fang, they can be on you with sticky fingers yanking at delicate fur.

How you deal with this potentially dangerous intrusion depends entirely on the origins of the kiddies. If the urchins are the prized offspring of your human's boss, it is best to ignore their invasion. Just hope the damage is minimal.

If, however, they are related or will never darken your abode again, scratch at will. It will be a life lesson they will never forget.

BEWARE! CAUTION! RUN!

Human babies are an especially dangerous lot. Avoid scratching, biting, or sleeping on them. Better yet just steer clear of them. Normally mild mannered adults turn violent if kitty gets too close to junior.

Even more sinister, their gift-wrapped bottoms hide a dangerous secret. If you spot steam rising from baby's rear area, run for the nearest exit.

I've known cats to launch themselves out of windows to escape the potentially fatal gaseous emanations. Fortunately, most landed on their feet.

Friendly Neighbors

Not all of us live in *Mr. Roger's Neighborhood.* We do, however, know neighbors who are special. It may be someone who builds you a shelter with Corinthian columns, who edges and mows lawns, or it may be just a friend to hang around with.

In my case, my special friendly neighbor is Miss Amy. She is an older feline, and sometimes she and I like to sit together and watch the leaves blow in the breeze. Special neighbors are the best. They make up for the ones that act like pests.

Family Time

Each day, set aside time to connect with your family. Just hang out in the same room with your people.

I like to spend time watching television in the evenings while I'm cuddled on someone's lap. I also like to snuggle with my cross-species brother before he gets out of bed in the morning.

The amount of time I spend with each person varies daily. By the end of a week, everyone has gotten an equal dose of fuzzy love.

Of course, this is another tactic calculated to enhance my status in the family unit. The more people who think I'm tops means the more people available to do my bidding at any given time. You can never have too many willing helpers stashed about.

The Renaissance Feline

Good breeding is not genetic, but it can be learned by the enterprising feline. A well-rounded cat is more than just a plump, furry lump. The refined cat is not only purrfectly coiffed, but also intellectually, socially, and artistically accomplished as well.

I focus on special activities that promote me as a cultured, entertaining, and poetic cat. It takes hard work, but as you rise like cream above the average feline, you will find yourself the object of envy and adoration.

Grooming

Good hygiene ranks at the top of my list when I think about the cats I want to spend time with. A sweet feline aroma should be all one smells within three feet of your body.

If your skin is crawling with lice, mites, or fleas, get treatment before social engagements. If your hair is matted, get a professional comb out. If smelly matter is stuck in your rear area, take a sudsy bath.

Your coat should be shiny, soft and lush. Your paws should be manicured and clean. Your behind should be unobtrusive in the olfactory sense. Do all three, and you are on your way to social success.

Clean between the toes and pads at least three times per week. Lint is lower class.

Social Graces

Thankfulness, a gesture most often associated with the niceties of social etiquette, is really another weapon in the arsenal of manipulation. Take time to learn how to use it well.

For example, this morning, just before my nap, I made a point of telling my chief male servant how much I appreciate his hard work and financial support.

With a gentle purr and a loving nudge, I sent him off to the salt mines to earn more tuna money. This small gesture brought a smile to his face as he trudged off to the bus in the dim light of dawn.

The act of being grateful is not natural to our species, but when you are a god living among men, you cannot completely ignore the emotional needs of the help. The occasional acknowledgment of their contributions to your care and comfort help our people to face the trials of their dreary existence.

The hope of a furry kiss, nudge, or gentle purr keeps the help going day after day after day. It practically compels humans to bend over backwards to make us happy.

That's enough about the help. Graciousness is a golden aura of thanks, goodness, and love that blinds others to your mistakes and faults. Cultivate and bask in its glow.

Do make sure someone witnesses your good works. Expending the effort while alone is nothing but a waste of quality napping time.

Each day I find time to give thanks. Taking my lead from popular culture, I have started a gratitude journal. The entries, addressed to the Allmeowty God, are questions I ponder, gracious thanks for beautiful things, or memories of special events in which I starred.

People always remember if you are a grateful, thankful, and gracious creature. Do not underestimate the power of this simple fact. Use it to your advantage.

Most Humbly Yours: A Personal Diary

Dear Allmeowty God,
When you created tinned fish you were right on the mark. By the way can you direct me to the closest fishing grounds? I just ordered a magnetic net. I have plans. Humbly, Me

Dear Allmeowty,
Thanks for the warm rays of sunshine. I do so love to nap in the warm glow. It gives me an angelic aura, which comes in handy on days I have been a bad kitty. Purrfectly, Me

Dear Allmeow,
Thank you for pretty flowers. I love to sit among them and spy on the neighbors. They make me smell good too. Sweetly, Me

Dear Al,
I do so love my catnip. Could I be addicted? I can stop anytime, I'm sure, but I just don't want to. It is true such pleasures are sinful? I pray catnip is kosher in the religious sense because Mommy bought me more today. Gotta Go!!! Me

Entertaining Recipes

The average feline has abysmal taste in food. Most think a bowl full of kibble and plain water makes a fine meal. I beg to differ.

Feline cuisine can be fresh, innovative, and tasty. I am including several elegant recipes that will make you the envy of every cat on the block.

Try something new every week. By the end of the year you will be a changed cat. For best results leave this section of the book open for the help to read.

Kitty Grocery List

Fish, Fish, Fish,
Fish, Fish, Fish,
Fish, Fish, Fish,
Catnip!!!

Fat Mice Grill With A Sizzle:
A Guide to Feline Cuisine

The first step to gourmet delight is a well-stocked pantry. I like to keep a dozen tins of albacore tuna, one tin of sardines, and one tin of salmon on hand at all times. I also devote one section to expensive kibble and canned liver pate'. I store fresh fish in the refrigerator, and the freezer generally holds a chicken or two at the ready should I desire fowl.

Fishy Stew
1 tin albacore tuna
Open tin pour contents in a bowl

Tuna Pizza
1 tin albacore tuna drained
1 cardboard pizza box
Open tin and drain
Arrange tuna to look like pizza

The Power of the Poet

Have you ever noticed how people love poetry? Purring verse you have written is the pinnacle of feline romanticism. Cuddly, furry romantics are especially attractive. If you want to be a winner, you would be wise to put pen to paper or, in my case, paw to computer.

Unleash the power of the poet. Bare your fuzzy soul. Look around. There are many wonderful things to spark creativity. Personally, I look to everyday life for inspiration, especially my life.

My preferred format is haiku. It's exotic, it's intellectual, but above all, it's short. You will notice working your way to the top requires hours of commitment. Save time where you can.

Here is an excerpt from my forthcoming book of poetry:

BEATNIK CAT: It's All About Me

EGOMANICAT
Know Cat's Ambition
Mission –Train All to Serve Me
Universe I Rule

CLEANCAT
Lick, Lick, Groom, Comb, Scrub
Kiss Me I Smell So Pretty
Kitties Lick Their Butts

SOPHISTICAT
Tuxedo Kitty
Formally Dressed White Boots, Gloves
Waiting For Invite

ITCHYCAT
Flea Ferry Mayday
Sophisticat Infested
Fleas Ignore Class Bounds

SUMMERCAT
Fine Fur Blows Through Air
Dandelions Don't Compare
Shedding Season's Here

ALTRUISTICAT
Scratch My Chin, Head, Neck
Humans Feeling Useful Smile
Cat Charity Work

MOGULCAT
Mine Rub, Mine Rub, Mine
House and Outdoors All Mine Too
I Own All I See

HUNGRYCAT
Tuna Cans Stacked High
Can Opener Purrs Loudly
Hurry, It's For Me

DRUGGIECAT
Fuzzy Green Mouse Flies
Sopping, Dripping Wet Toy Mouse
Catnip Fuels My Play

LANDLORDCAT
Sparrows Build Love Nest
Little Birdies Are You Warm?
Purrhaps, I Should Check?

MUSECAT
I Am My Own Muse
Amusing As That May Seem
I Inspire Myself

Feline Philanthropy

Charitable acts or acts of kindness can enhance your community standing while, at the same time, helping others less fortunate. I personally choose to give up two tins of tuna per month and use the savings to support some of my favorite charities.

I support local spay and neuter clinics, no kill shelters, and the local humane society. Further, I am a strong proponent of rodent feeding programs (for obvious reasons).

The important point to remember is that it does not matter how much or how little you give, as long as you receive public recognition for your good deeds. Anonymous giving may benefit the recipient, but does very little to enhance one's social status, which, of course, is the primary point.

Polite Conversation

Another way to squelch the competition and enhance your social reputation is to cultivate exceptional conversational skills. Intelligent conversation attracts intelligent companions. An elite attitude results in friends of the same stature.

When you speak like a king, you exude a kingly attitude. This makes it all the more likely you will be treated royally as well.

As a favor to your edification, I am including some of my more erudite phraseology. Add these to your conversations and watch yourself rise to the pinnacle of the social elite.

Also, try to avoid mixing with the wrong crowd. Of course, when you are kicking back with a sour milk at the local bar or hanging out with your pals, it is unlikely the Queen of Sheba will waltz through the door. In this situation, a resounding, "Well, slap my buttocks!" is not out of place as an exclamation.

As a rule, pay attention to the time, the place and the situation. The smart cat modifies his or her behavior to each and every social situation.

I dare say!

This phrase can be used for emphasis at the beginning or end of a sentence. For example, "I dare say! This tuna tastes off."

For gosh sakes!

Again, this a useful phrase to convey shock, surprise or disgust. For example, "For gosh sakes! The last time I was this insulted, I was informed I suffered from common ear mites!"

Nudges, purrs and butterfly kisses.

Polite society abhors unnecessary body contact. Hollywood stars have perfected the art of the air kiss. This is the feline equivalent which can be used either as a greeting or when you leave a social engagement. "Chloe darling, the fish was divine. Let's do lunch." Nudges, purrs and butterfly kisses!

Advice for the Ages

Like "Dear Abby" I am often asked to comment on difficult situations and social etiquette. I am including some of the more poignant problems I have encountered.

I am sure either you or servants will recognize these universal predicaments. Sometimes it is easier to see yourself through someone else's plight.

From the Mouths of Cats:

Dear Dr. Catman,

I am a country mouser. I'd like to impress the ladies at the next hoedown. What do you suggest?

Barn Cat

Dear Mouser,

First, I trust your desire to meet women is purely platonic. Spay and neuter responsibly, I always say. Second, I'd suggest you bathe thoroughly and roll vigorously in clover before the dance. Finally, avoid sleeping with pigs, cows, or sheep for a week prior. Good luck.

Dr. Catman

Dear Dr. Catman,

My neighbor has three koi in the pond in their back yard. I'm craving a little sashimi, but they have a big dog guarding their yard. What should I do?

Fishy Cat

Dear Fishy Cat,

This is one of those situations where self-restraint is the best option. Remember koi are overgrown goldfish. They may look pretty, but their flesh is tougher than nails. No need to risk life and limb for that. You may, however, enjoy taunting the guard by walking just outside the fence line and watching the dolt bolt into the boards. Now that's entertainment. Satisfy that fish craving with a tin of sardines.

Dr. Catman

Dear Dr. Catman,

I recently dreamed I was in a noisy, crowded place listening to old Elvis tunes. Suddenly three 7's appeared before me and coins fell on my head. What does this mean?

Lucky Cat

Dear Lucky Cat,

Sometimes dreams can be prophetic. I believe a trip to Las Vegas is in order. I see riches in your future. Remember to pack a hard hat.

Dr. Catman

Dear Dr. Catman,

I aspire to be a pampered pet living in a four-star home. My current family believes hot dogs are haute cuisine. My palate suffers, and I am gaining weight from all the fat in the franks.

Miss Chloe

Dear Miss Chloe,

I can tell you are a refined feline. Are you Siamese purrhaps? My advice is to pack your bags, call a cab and relocate to the nearest luxury penthouse. Caviar, not weenies, is your destiny.

Dr. Catman

The Help Need Help Too!

Dear Dr. Catman,

I spent big money on a deluxe, three-story, scratching post hangout for my tabby. I hoped it might spare my furniture from nightly attack. So far, no luck, although kitty does enjoy pouncing on me from on high.

Scratched

Dear Scratched,

Your cat is fine. You, however, need to rethink your selfish attitude. Felines own all items in their territory. Your claim is merely monetary; the furniture belongs to your cat. Stop worrying and be glad kitty is happy. Your next step is probably therapy. Narcissism is a psychiatric issue.

Dr. Catman

Dear Dr. Catman,

My social life is in tatters. My puss has driven everyone away. Each time I have a visitor, kitty stalks them like prey. The only warning before imminent attack is a low rumbling akin to thunder. Few suspect it is feline in origin until too late. My last visitor was chased into an upstairs bedroom and cowered behind a locked door without access to food, water or facilities for 10 hours. All the while, Mr. Snookums howled, hissed and scratched at the door. After I got home, my friend bolted, never to return. What is wrong with my cat?

Lonely and Perplexed

Dear Lonely and Perplexed,

I dare say, Mr. Snookums is a hero. He is obviously sensing the aberrant nature of your friends and family. No doubt he's saved you numerous times from felonious assault, or even death at the hand of the psychos you invite into your home. Have puss pre-screen all visitors. No doubt you choose only strange and dangerous people for company. Give kitty a pat on the back and a case of tuna. He's saved your neck many times over and deserves a treat.

Dr. Catman

Dear Dr. Catman,

Kitty Cat, a stray I've been feeding for years, recently moved onto my back porch. Yesterday, I noticed a foul odor and found a pile of kitty poo under his favorite chair. What does this mean?

Proprietor Cat Café

Dear Proprietor Cat Café,

Kudos to Mr. Cat. He's taken action to change his life and become an indoor puss. As for the poo issue, this is a cry for help if ever I've seen one. Give the poor man his own office. In the greater scheme of things, what's a little kitty litter, a box, and a scoop going to set you back? Indulge the old puss. He probably won't last much longer anyway. Won't you feel better in the end if you pamper him a bit now? Run, don't walk, to that porch and get him set up today. You may already be too late.

Dr. Catman

The advice I dispense changes lives every day. Each night I fall asleep knowing I'm somebody's hero. That is the greatest feeling in the world.

Now if I could just reach a wider audience. Purrhaps a television talk show is the ticket.

Creative License

As you can see, the best solutions to everyday problems demand creativity. Only you can know what level of work or what methods work best in your family or in your neighborhood. Follow my suggestions, test the techniques, and modify your approach to suit your own needs.

I dare say, it's no wonder we catş sleep so much, considering the machinations we go through for our most basic comforts. Oops…it's time for my afternoon nap!

Epilogue

Today, I am living the life of a king. I dare say, if someone of my humble beginnings can do it, you can too. If I can change one feline's life, I will be a happy man.

Of course I've already changed my life, so I guess I'm ahead of the game. Meows and swats to you, and good luck.

Let me know how you make out. Remember to write me with your success stories. It will give me fodder for another book.

Each of us possesses the ability to improve our lives. Follow my lead and reach for the stars.

Get started today! And, finally, stay out of my territory. I rule here.

Nudges, Purrs, and Whisker Kisses,
Dr. Catman, M.E.C.A.T.
www.beatnikcat.com

Printed in the United States
18246LVS00006B/1-168